INSPIRATIONAL STORIES OF THE HOMELESS

Dignity, Nobility, Decency

Michael Williams

i

THANK YOU FOR YOUR INVESTMENT IN
THIS BOOK. YOU CAN LOCATE OTHER
BOOKS BY THIS AUTHOR AT
WWW.AMAZON.COM OR FOLLOW THIS
AUTHOR FOR NEW EDITIONS, NEW BOOKS,
SPEAKING ENGAGEMENTS AND SPECIAL
EVENTS

Published by
Dysfunctional Child Publishing
williamsmike4171930@gmail.com
San Diego, California

First Printing, 2016
Printed in the United States of America

ISBN: 10: 0692626921
ISBN-13: 978-0692626924

DEDICATION

This book is dedicated to those who are
without homes and continue to pursue their
dreams, and for my creator.
"I am not home!"

ACKNOWLEDGMENTS

I gratefully acknowledge the inspiration of Wendy Dan, L.C.S.W., Maya Klein, Ph.D., and Leila Rhodes, M.D., who are brilliant healers.

Thank you!

CONTENTS

Preface

PREFACE

These are stories about the better side of the human experience that carries on in the midst of unrestrained cruelties. How does one obtain or maintain dignity without a place to lay one's head? How does one be noble when hungry? How does one be decent when cold and wet? Yet, people do!

Is a soup kitchen different from anywhere else when it comes to being human? There is the occasional drunk, the hungry, the short-tempered, the under-employed, mental illness, occasional death, the disabled, physical illness, the ex-con, and more. Does this environment challenge our humanity?

I have observed gentility, kindness, sacrifice, patience, and compassion in the face of brutality while passing out bag lunches amid the homeless. These are stories of nobility that deserve to be told. These are stories of wisdom.

Here are stories of the human spirit which in some way continued to grow, not in spite of homelessness but sometimes because of homelessness.

FIRST STORY

A SOUP KITCHEN, BAG LUNCHES, AND DIGNITY

The most important thing soup kitchens do is empower people! This may be surprising considering most kitchens feed, shelter, and clothe hundreds.

Empowerment occurs in indistinguishable, minute steps; like any other human growth, it is the process of life. Without developmental empowerment humanity does not progress, and progress has and will always be the undeniable goal of generations.

This is not a story of having all the answers or doing it perfectly; rather it is a story of the subtle nuances of human learning and development.

The mission of most soup kitchens is to serve the low-income, homeless, and the underserved. Most concentrate on food, basic needs, family and social services, employment, children and youth. Many also distribute bag lunches as the homeless are walking out the door. While you may not suspect the bag lunches serve a valuable purpose, they do.

I am an honorably discharged homeless veteran. I hand out bag lunches to the homeless daily as a volunteer. When I was first given this task I was instructed to give one lunch to each person as he or she leaves the morning breakfast. In addition to food, the soup kitchen provides showers along with laundry services.

Being thoroughly trained to follow orders I did as instructed; however with time I got to know the people, and as with all relationships, with knowledge comes understanding, which leads to tolerance, which leads to compassion. It was this sense of being able to feel the pain of the people I was asked to serve that led to my own internal development of empathy.

Prior to this I must reservedly admit my attitude was to do as I had been told and give one lunch to each person. When people asked for two lunches, emotionally I responded sometimes with suspicion as opposed to tolerance and an attempt to understand.

As I got to know the people, relationships developed; and as they did I got to learn the needs of the individuals. They were no longer the homeless. They were Hector, Denise, Susan, Gwendolyn, Jose, Karen, and Sam and they were people with whom I was in relationships with, who had needs. I could no longer like a robot hand out a bag lunch to each individual as they came by regardless of their needs or situation.

I came to realize that my behavior could be more responsive to the demands of the needs of the people I was asked to serve, as opposed to requesting the needs of the homeless to be respectful to the rules I was asked to enforce. Often those rules were not responsive to the needs I saw before me. They empowered me as opposed to empowering those who were in need. I came to experience the needs of the people I served as I was able to allow myself to experience some of their pain and vulnerability. I attempt to share some of those experiences with you here.

What impressed me most at the beginning of this experience was that eighty percent of the people who came through the soup kitchen got their one lunch and left. To a great degree this story is about the other twenty percent.

Occasionally, someone would ask for two lunches and I always said no. Then one woman who asked said to me, "I have a job for ten hours today and I will be paid fifty dollars cash at the end of the day. Can you give me two bags, one for lunch and dinner?" I did. The next day when I saw her I suspected she was going to ask for two lunches again; she did not. She gazed into my eyes and said, "Only one lunch please, I have all I need today." In that moment I realized she was at peace. She had the one thing some of us spend a life-time in search of: peace. I was envious. Occasionally she still asks for two lunches, and on those days I know she has work. She has been an example for me of how to walk through vulnerability and to be at peace and comfort within.

The second person who impressed me was a man who each day would ask for three lunches. He would explain he had children at home and they were for them and one was allergic to peanuts many of our lunches are peanut butter and jelly. Once again, I responded with suspicion as opposed to tolerance. Then a few days later I saw him eating breakfast with what looked like the cutest kids on the planet, his nine-year-old daughter and ten-year-old son. My suspicions had been wrong. Now whenever I see him I automatically give him three lunches whenever the children are not around and I try to search for any sandwich other than peanut butter for his daughter. I realize, like most nine, and ten-year-olds they want to sleep in during the summer vacation.

Hopefully, the lunches provides some semblance of a normal childhood for his children.

Then there are the working poor. There are many people who work for minimum wage or less and all their resources go to just maintain housing and there is nothing left for food. I have come to learn these are the people most likely to ask for two bags. They use one for lunch and the other for dinner. I can certainly sympathize with working all day and being in fear of no dinner.

There is one couple, let's call them Bill and Maria for anonymity purposes who sleep in the local park. They sit together every day. One day he started to come in without her and also started to ask for two lunches. By now I had begun to learn, so I gave him two. The next day, I asked, "Where is Maria?" and he replied, She is still sleeping in the park. She has a cold."

Sometimes there are people with certain food allergies so the lunches may be inappropriate for them that day, so on those days they go hungry. Then there are those without teeth. On days when we have apples, or pears, or anything that requires teeth, they go hungry.

In retrospect, I wish I had been more trusting

in the beginning. Most of the homeless who ask for two or three lunches have very good reasons for doing so, and I find it amazing that in a homeless population so few do ask. I do not know if I have that kind of faith in my creator. From the homeless I have learned lessons of faith and peace.

Don't misunderstand my intentions here. It is not to paint a picture of piety within this population, for there are the deceitful, the devious, and the tricksters, as with all populations. However I think it more challenging to remain faithful when one is without shelter and food.

In this task of handing out bag lunches each day I have learned a valuable lesson. I have learned that it is not simply a bag of food. It is something more important than that. It is some semblance of dignity and all creation deserves dignity. It is an inherent right of all creatures to be valued and respected.

On those occasions when I responded with suspicion as opposed to tolerance, I was not respecting the inherent value of human beings to make decisions with respect to their needs; I was not responding with respect nor allowing dignity. I have learned that bag lunches often are, in effect, distributions of dignity.

When a father can go back to the hotel with a couple of bags of food for his children he has some semblance of dignity and it allows some semblance of a childhood for his children. When a man can go back to the park with a bag of food for his beloved girlfriend who is sleeping on the ground trying to recover from a cold, in that bag is a small semblance of dignity. When a woman who is working all day for less than minimum wage and we give her two bags of food that allow her the ability to work then there is dignity. When someone who has no teeth searches for applesauce and it is given, they have dignity.

There are many more stories told here. However I hope this one will show that dignity is important and makes a difference to one of our creator's most vulnerable populations.

SECOND STORY

SCULPTING OUR HUMANITY

I watched a homeless gentleman at the morning breakfast at the soup kitchen today. He was carefully carving off small pieces of chicken and placing them in his mouth for what appeared to be an unusually long period of time to chew such a small piece of food. He ate very deliberately. He has no teeth. I will never be able to fully know the experience of attempting to nourish oneself without the benefit of teeth. However I imagine it is a hardship, especially when one does not have the advantage of choosing one's own food. Watching this gentleman gave me gratitude. I am grateful for teeth.

I noted the grass on his pants legs and back, and once again I was grateful because the night before I had slept in a bed while he slept in the park with a blanket on top of him that was now tied to his back-pack.

He pulled out four different medications and took each one while taking a small sip of water. I was grateful again because I have immediate access to water.

As a result of my conversations with this gentleman I feel as if I know important things about him. I know he has not always been homeless. I know he has a story that led to where he is today. I know there were many things beyond his control.

I know his life is a struggle. I know some of the struggles of his life. I know that I have things like teeth, a bed, and access to water and he does not. I know sometimes he is awoken at night because the rats amass in the park where the homeless congregate; as they sleep, the animals search for any food that may be in their midst. I know when he wakes up in the morning his first challenge is to find a toilet, thus his daily trips to the soup kitchen for the restroom and showers made available to the homeless. His next challenge for the day is food, and once again, the soup kitchen steps in to provide. Depending upon what is served he may or may not be able to eat since he has no teeth. Then he has the challenge of lunch later in the day and once again the soup kitchen is there. He wakes up around 4:30 am to be at the kitchen at 5:30 am since the walk from the park to the kitchen is a distance.

What do I know about this gentleman? I know that by 7:30 am he has endured more hardship than most of us. I know his life must have significant anxiety from things like being able to find water to take medications. I know he has to walk over a mile to use the toilet, to eat, and to shower. I know sometimes when he finds food it will be to no avail. I know the grass on his clothes comes not from lack of care but from lack of resources.

From this knowledge comes understanding for what most of us would label an unkempt appearance. From this understanding comes increased tolerance for the veracity of his circumstances; from tolerance comes empathy, and from empathy comes compassion.

As with all things, compassion for the homeless comes with paradoxes. There is a part of me that would like to tell him what to do; however, there is also an awareness that I have no blueprint to tell him anything of what to do because I lack enough real-world experience, knowledge, understanding, and skill of his reality to be helpful. I would be guessing at best and it would not even be a well-informed guess. So, I am left to struggle with my own humility or lack thereof, my own limitation of understanding, and my own sense of powerlessness, and therein I imagine must be some sense of his reality, humility or lack thereof, limitations of understanding and powerlessness.

I have come to realize it can be two things that compel me to want to make a difference in this man's life. The first is a true compassion that makes me yearn to make a difference. The second is an inability to accept my own discomfort in realizing that there but for the grace of a benevolent creator go I. It is easier for me to instruct, which gives an illusion of control, rather than accept my own distress, which may inform me of my own vulnerability. It becomes a perplexing paradox at best, which may be the essence of the human struggle.

Maybe the homeless have an endowment for us. They remind us of our humanity. They strike a chord in each of us to be kind, charitable, to have sympathy, to have mercy, to acquire understanding, and to act with tolerance and compassion, since to see the pain of those on the streets without wanting to make a difference would be heartless. Maybe the essence of humanity is in part our compassion for our own vulnerabilities.

The homeless bequeath us the gifts of charity, sympathy, kindness, tolerance, mercy, and compassion by simply being who they are. Being who they are allows us to foster the best within us and to bring that forward in action. So if we respond by giving to the homeless, who has given the greater gift, the donor or the homeless? Maybe the essence of our humanity is in the questions for which there are no easy answers.

In this moment, you can choose to be who you choose to be; we do have a choice. We can embrace any procrastination, critique, contempt or withdrawal we may feel for those whose journey may be different than maybe your own or we can choose to respond with compassionate action.

Decide to make a difference, yes, for the compassion of those in a reality of uncertainty, to say the least, but more importantly to sculpt your own humanity.

THIRD STORY

THE POWER OF A ZIP LOCK BAG

The other day, I was handing out bag lunches at the soup kitchen. The volunteers who pack the lunches had run out of brown paper bags, so some of the lunches were in those clear large zip lock transparent bags. I noted two things concerning this occurrence. The first was that those who came for a lunch were pleased they could immediately see what was inside. Like most of us, the homeless want to have some choice in what they eat. I suspect some element of choice gives us a sense of some control in our lives. Maybe we all need a little of that for any degree of emotional stability. Secondly, and maybe more importantly, is the fact that on that day there was a mixture of both brown paper bags lunches and lunches in the see-through zip lock plastic. A large percentage of the people preferred the see through zip lock lunches. I asked a gentleman, "So, you like what you see inside?" He replied, "No, I want the zip lock bag."

Then I looked around the soup kitchen and most folks had multiple bags in their possession. There were backpacks, shopping bags, plastic bags, paper bags, small bags, large bags, tent bags, tool bags, duffle bags, garbage bags, shoulder bags, any bag imaginable. The average homeless person had a minimum of three or four bags.

When one is homeless, portability of one's possessions and daily necessities is a critical skill to master for survival. This is the reason the gentleman who answered my question that day answered as he did. He realized the bag was as valuable as the contents. It could be washed out and reused for food each day. There are always a multitude of people who have disposable Tupperware containers and/or bags, and they fill them with food for later in the day.

For most of us, we could hardly ever imagine that one of the most valuable things that a soup kitchen can distribute is a clear zip lock plastic bag. However, bags are an indispensable tool of survival for the homeless. A variety of bags provides an opportunity for folks in a precarious situation to exercise choices and effectively plan and organize for example some diabetics need some form of bag that can contain ice for insulin. This process is crucial to survival. At soup kitchens we see things others do not; or may not deem important. That is, unless you are homeless and you are forced to go hungry because you do not have that one bag or container that would have allowed you to plan and organize your food for the day. There are few among us who would have seen what the homeless gentleman saw in the moment he requested the lunch in the zip lock bag.

His request demonstrated honesty, humility, and courage. He asked for a lunch in a zip lock bag because that was the reality of his needs.

None of us alone can end the pain of homelessness; however we can choose to not let what we cannot do prevent us from doing what we can do. We can demonstrate the honesty, humility, and courage of the homeless man described above and do what we can in this moment to diminish the pain of homelessness. Make a difference today and enjoy the authenticity of your own honesty, humility, and courage. You will instantly feel more whole and loving in the process, because you will be honoring your own need to do what you can!

Imagine how powerful your making a difference is compared to the power of a zip lock bag!

FOURTH STORY

A SOUP KITCHEN, BONDING, AND APPLE PIE

From the beginning of humanity much of the human experience has been dependent upon communication, community, and collaboration. Without these, we lack much of what we value most: being in relationship.

At soup kitchens, one may not suspect communication, community, and collaboration are nurtured, but they are. Among the homeless, before, during, and after the morning breakfast there is community. There is valuable and effective communication through sharing throughout the community. There is an invariable allocation of the know-how necessary to survive on the streets. There develops a collaboration that supports continued existence for many souls, especially the newly homeless who are quite defenseless. I now understand the concept of community in a more meaningful way.

Many of the homeless who eat at the morning breakfast start to gather ninety minutes before the meal is served. Yes, some come for the coffee, free showers, and free laundry; however there are many who gather particularly for the sense of community. This is a subtle nuance, but when we look closely it is there. I share one occasion.

An unforgettable moment I observed was watching banter between two homeless women. They were having a chat on the numerous ways to bake an apple pie. Off the top, one would not suspect this chat held significant meaning. However I experienced it otherwise. First, what I observed in these women was a moment in their lives when each of them knew the quality of the apple pie they fashioned made the people they loved happy. These women debated everything from crusts, to seasonings, to varieties of apples. One stressed the use of Jonagold and Winesap apples, while the other woman thought a combination of Crispin and Granny Smith apples made for a superb texture all the way through the pie. They discussed the importance of using fresh butter for a properly golden crust, and using the right combination of butter and flour for a superb crust. These women held an ardent pride in what they once were, or, from listening to them, still are, because in my heart of hearts I suspect they could still bake like Martha Stewart if they had an oven and a home. One of them even told of taking her baking skills commercial to local businesses, barber shops, bakeries, and entering the state fair. Obviously, this is a woman who once was the best of the best when it comes to baking.

I enjoyed listening to the account of the smiles they put on the faces of their loved ones during those times and their envy of their grandmothers who passed along their baking secrets and bequeathed a legacy. One woman told of perfecting her grandmother's recipe over years and then when she thought she had got it just right she went to see her grandmother with a pie. She gave her grandmother a slice of pie and said, "Grandma, I made this pie just like you used to." Her grandmother tasted it, looked at her, and casually replied, "Baby, I never made a pie like that; but you got close." The women chuckled, as so did I. These women reminded me of the apple pies I once ate as my grandmother watched, and once more I smelled the bouquet of apple pies long since gone.

I saw a shared pride between two women who once upon a time were like any other women sharing a family recipe. It was a time in their lives where they felt usefulness, fulfillment, need, togetherness, community, and relationships. I wondered what happened along their journey. I respect their ability to bear the burdens they must carry. I admire their power to endure. Most of all, I am in awe of their capacity to carry on as best they can each day. They touch me in a way I am not often touched.

Listening to these women reminded me they were not always homeless. There was a time when each had a home, family, traditions, and rituals of value to communicate love. These women share something most of us will never speak of. They share tremendous loss!

As I listened, it felt as if each would give

anything to bake one more apple pie for those they lost along the way. It was not so much what they were sharing as it was the tone of their reminiscences that made me feel they were longing for times that would never come again. In that moment I felt for them. They share a connection. On the surface their chat appears to be about apple pie, however they also share remembrances of the loss of a life which was once esteemed.

The conversation of baking apple pie could have happened anywhere. The shared sentiment, understanding, empathy, and knowing looks between them could only have occurred at a soup kitchen.

One woman told the other, "Well, those were certainly good times." I realized their reminiscence was heightened by their connection, not in spite of their homelessness; but because of their homelessness, and that is one of the most valuable contributions soup kitchens make to the homeless they provide a sense of community to those who are ostracized from community. We may have sympathy for those who have lost home, family, and friends, however empathy can only be shared among those of like experience. Try as we may, the experience of homelessness and what leads to it cannot be emulated.

One of these women lives in her car with all her possessions. The other lives on the streets and carries her belongings in a cart. They are linked in the most pragmatic way.

Choose to make a difference and help those who now live on the streets to share memories of apple pie.

FIFTH STORY

HOMELESS CHILDREN EAT FIRST

Children eat first is one of the most prevailing customs among the homeless community!

As families come into the morning breakfast at soup kitchens with children for the first time, it is always interesting to watch the homeless community respond.

As a new family walks into the room, those standing in the food line will always suggest, "Children go to the front of the line." The parents of the children are frequently surprised with this code of conduct. It is always pleasing to see a whole family move to the front of the line.

This etiquette is unforeseen, considering the people sending the families to the front of the line are hungry. It is not unusual among the homeless to hear the words, "I have not eaten in over a day," or "I have not eaten in two days." It is the norm. Yet it is the hungry that advocate sending children to the front of the line.

A new family came into the room for the first

time with five children. Several homeless people informed the parents that children go to the front of the line, but there was firm resistance from the parents as the family went to the back of the line to wait their turn. I overheard one of the parents make the comment, "We're not special so we'll wait like everyone else." Over the next few days, with a graceful gentility I have rarely seen, the homeless community persuaded the parents it would be best for all involved for the children to go to the front of the line.

It was a heartwarming moment in the community the first time this family acquiesced to the practice, and there were pleasant smiles throughout the food line as we all viewed five stair-step children standing at the front of the line.

In a couple more days, not only were all the children standing in the front of the line, but they were standing there with their parents. The community had brought the newly homeless, who are at risk the most, into the flock.

The children's ages are 16, 14, 12, 10, and 7. Now the only challenge that remained was recognition, since the 12-year-old and the 10-year-old are of similar height and weight and they both have shoulder-length blond hair. When they are standing together folks often refer to them as "you girls," and in response the 12-year-old always yells, "I'm a boy." Luckily, the remaining boys are all readily identifiable as boys. I guess no community is without its challenges.

One of the pleasant things about morning breakfast at most soup kitchens is people can go through the line as many times as necessary to eat as much as they need. One morning I saw the 16-year-old boy go back through the line for a third time (16-year-old boys are apparently very hungry). His 10-year-old sister had been sitting next to him. As he was waiting in line, his sister casually eyed the food that was remaining on his tray. She looked to her right, looked to her left, looked at her brother in line, and then slowly started eating his eggs. I guess she did not want to get up to get her own. Fortunately, when her brother returned he never noticed her kind assistance. As she looked backward and realized I had observed what she had done, we shared a smile and quiet laugh, unbeknownst to those around us. Her brother does not know how generous he was that day.

The baby boy often has his favorite stuffed animal with him. He typically is the first to grab a bag lunch and enjoys taking one lunch at a time until he has acquired seven lunches for the whole family. I have no idea why he enjoys making seven trips, however it makes him happy and it is all about doing whatever it takes to make a 7-year-old homeless child happy. Coincidentally, fruit also makes him happy, especially oranges or tangerines. I have often observed the other children in the family giving him their oranges or tangerines.

When the oldest boy comes for sack lunches, he makes it a point to get one for each member of the family all at the same time.

There is nothing more tenderly poignant than to be an onlooker at the range of homeless people rifling through their own sack lunches and taking out a sandwich, piece of fruit, or bag of chips and placing it on the table for this family of seven.

There are countless children who pass through the food line during the morning breakfast, and with each smiling face of a homeless child the community at the breakfast becomes more vulnerable. Maybe we need the least of us to remind us who we really are.

Sometimes the 10-year-old will come to me for lunches (the only girl) and ask, "May I have three lunches, one for me and two for my oldest brother?" I guess there is nothing wrong with a little girl looking out for her oldest brother.

There have been times that this small, thin-as-a-rail, 10-year-old girl has extended her arms while holding out both her hands cupped together, gazed into my eyes with a remarkable innocence, and said, "May I have a sack lunch please?"

So I want you to now imagine this thin-as-a-rail little girl in her Converse high-top sneakers with no socks, dress that is two sizes too small, with arms and legs that go on forever, with shadowy circles under her eyes, and she is now reaching out to you with both her hands cupped together while gazing in your eyes and asking, "May I have a lunch please?" It is your kindness and charity that allows any community to reach back and say, "Yes, you can."

SIXTH STORY

SO LITTLE, SO HAPPY

One of the most valuable aspects of any soup kitchen is the electrical outlets. So many folks come for food, shelter, and clothes that often the electrical outlets are overlooked as a resource, other than by the homeless. A cell phone provides access to resources necessary for climbing out of homelessness. Without recharging the phone, however, it is worthless. Each morning at breakfast there are those who come in to charge their phones. Sometimes it takes so little to make some so happy.

One of the volunteers during the morning breakfast puts up chairs, returns trays to the kitchen, and empties the garbage. As a result, he always has those large black garbage bags. Almost daily someone will ask him for a garbage bag, not because they have a home to use it in, but because it is needed to carry all their worldly possessions. A garbage bag for those asking serves a critical function, because it carries all the acquired treasures of a life-time. Sometimes it takes so little to make some so happy.

A gentleman who eats daily comes into the soup kitchen with a bag of clothes. He asks those present if anyone needs clothes and several say no because the clothes are too small. The bag consists of two men's tee-shirts and two pairs of men's slacks that are old but serviceable and clean.

He then asks if I know anyone who might benefit from the clothes. I reply I am sure I will find someone, and right at that moment a woman walks up to us and says, "I need clothes." She looks in the bag, pulls out each shirt and comments, "This will fit perfectly." Then she reviews the slacks with the same comment again.

She hurries back to the showers while shouting, "I am going to get cleaned up and put on my new outfit." Later she reappears and poses for us who have witnessed what transpired, and we all remark how good she looks. She is rather proud of herself!

To most, receiving two used tee-shirts and two pairs of slacks may not be an occasion, however in her case the only clothes she owned were the ones on her back. As she walked away that day she carried her bag of clothes while commenting, "I can change clothes whenever I want now." She was as happy as I have ever seen a human being.

Sometimes it takes so little to make some so happy.

There is a husband and wife who come to the soup kitchen morning breakfast a couple times a week with their three children. The children are in the third, fourth, and sixth grades; two girls and a boy in the middle. As they enter the building the mother always picks up a lunch for each member of the family. They sit down and eat breakfast together and she once commented to me, "Thank you, it is so important that the children have a good hot breakfast before going to school." When finished the entire family hurries off to get the kids to school on time.

What I find amazing about this family is not their gratitude for the breakfast or the lunches. What is astounding is being able to watch as they sit together as a family, often rearranging chairs or tables to do so. I observe their interactions with one another. Careful caresses the mother makes to each child, stroking hair, touching arms, or the smiles she gently gives each. The husband makes several trips during the breakfast to replenish cups of milk for the children or coffee for him and his wife.

What I think I perceive when watching this family is "family!" I hope that makes sense. I have been in many exclusive homes, but it is in witnessing these individuals who are part of the working poor that I detect the truest sense of family. If I had to guess, and I shall, it appears that what this family values most above all else is being together. Sometimes it takes so little to make some so happy.

SEVENTH STORY

NEWLY HOMELESS MOTHER AND SONS

It is 5:30-A.M. The sun is not quite up and a mother stands with her nine-year-old son clinging to her body. Her left arm is wrapped around his shoulders. Her five-year-old son is on the other side of her body clinging to his mama's thigh. All of them are holding on tightly, occasionally squeezing as if to assure one another they are still there.

The mother has three towels draped over her shoulders and her long black hair gently caresses the towels. They all have the exact same facial features and beautiful dark-olive skin. They are family.

I stare at the mother attempting to understand her; I cannot. She looks as if she is making an effort to be strong while holding back tears. Occasionally, one tear escapes and slowly trickles down her cheek, dropping onto the face of her eldest son. He looks surprised as he wipes away the tear and looks up at his mother in bewilderment. They both smile as she apologizes.

This is the face of the newly homeless waiting to use the showers.

It is hard to picture the feelings surging through this mother. The questions she must be asking herself are probably overwhelming. The fears she must be feeling are almost certainly an avalanche cascading her heart. The eldest son appears to want to help, yet not knowing how; the youngest son simply appears to want to hold onto mama.

As hard as we try we will never be able to imagine how this mother is feeling at this moment unless we have been where she is. Our inability to imagine her pain, her suffering is our best evidence of our own blessings. If there is such a thing as terror, I suspect that is what the children are feeling now, terror, fear, confusion, loneliness, all wrapped up as an indescribable sting that most of us are afraid to touch.

It is agonizing to look at this mother and her sons; yet there is something strangely striking about it. It elicits an aching tenderness that is difficult to know what to do with. Her suffering lures and induces. I cannot look away, at the same time I long to look away. I do look away, yet I keep coming back. I want to pretend that this mother and sons are not there, they do not exist, yet they do.

As the devoted it is our job not to look away. Our job is to shoulder the sufferings the rest of humanity is shocked to look at. We will look at this family. We will provide showers for this family. We will feed this family. We will talk with this family, provide social services, and inquire how to be of assistance.

They may be on the streets, but it is our imperative not only to be of assistance but to make a difference in the lives of this one family who obviously has nowhere else to go.

The mother exits the showers with her two sons. She is in a black dress apparently ready to go to work, and each son is wearing black dress shoes and slacks with white shirts and ties and sweaters. To look at them now you would not know they were homeless. Their presentation is beyond reproach. An ordinary soup kitchen has made a difference.

All three enter the morning breakfast line. They go to the front of the line acquiescing to the tradition that children go to the front of the line. As they eat, occasionally someone puts a piece of fruit on the table where they are sitting. It is a contribution from the homeless to the homeless and a way that children in the community are continually recognized. It may not appear too much to those on the outside, however it is immense when one considers the folks making the donations are there because they do not have enough to eat.

This family starts to come daily. Later I learn all three sleep in the car at night. I wonder if the children get cold at night. It is aggravating that I do not know, but then again if I knew, what can I do? Sometimes the vulnerabilities of humanity are just vulnerabilities, and there is nothing that can be done, it is the kind of creatures that we are. Maybe that is why the mother and sons kept squeezing each other. Maybe sometimes in the midst of our vulnerabilities, all we can do is to assure each other that we are there, we are present, and we will not look away or run away.

After about a month I no longer see this family coming each day to the kitchen. Then one day the oldest son appears. He asks me for a sack lunch. I ask him about his brother and mother — they are on their way to work. I give him four lunches for the family. The children are out of school and they are all going to clean houses for the day.

Hector is one of my favorite people to see, although he is only nine years old. Pardon me; I momentarily forgot, nine and a half. I have learned that the half is just as important as the nine, per Hector's tutoring.

Several times a week Hector comes for lunches as his mother waits in the car and his brother sleeps in the car. Every day they go to clean houses. I am unsure how these young children may be of assistance in house-cleaning, but I am absolutely sure it is something the family has learned to do in order to survive.

There have been times I have given Hector a half-dozen lunches at a time. I have counseled him to always ask for what is needed. Even at nine he has an advanced maturity for his age, maybe because he has to in order to survive.

EIGHTH STORY

HUMILITY AND HOMELESSNESS

"Swinging for the fences" describes the intention of swinging for a home run. It requires more energy, more effort. With the vicissitudes of homelessness, energy tends to be in short supply; yet it is this force of power of swinging for the fences that is demonstrated each day by most of the homeless. It is especially poignant in homeless children and/or adolescents. The homeless day after day persistently construct a voluminous level of energy just to sustain survival. More remarkable is the paradox of how it intermingles with ordinary tasks. It emerges as an existence of accomplishing the dreary as if it has at its roots a spirit of nobility. For what can be nobler than survival?

It feels as if many of the children or adolescents who are homeless have an inner world that is somewhat detached, calm, maybe even peaceful, and a maturity beyond their years. They are keen observers. They calmly plan for the next vicissitude of being homeless, which generally will be within the next few hours.

It is attention-grabbing to watch a boy and his sister pack Tupperware for the required meals of the day. Their organization is meticulous; one can quickly tell they have done this a thousand times before. As adults we may feel a yearning to be of some support until we realize these young folks know what they are doing. In their world is a multitude of experiences of hunger that have evolved into a wealth of knowledge and skills. Their chiseled wisdom for survival exceeds many well-meaning adults'. Therefore as adults we need to maintain a level of respect for this acquired knowledge evolved from a situation we may be unfamiliar with. Given these circumstances, the best thing a well-meaning adult can do is to ask the question: "Is there any way I can be of assistance to you?"

It may be challenging for many to admit in this situation these youth may know more of what they are doing than most of us ever will. In this situation many well-intentioned adults have little, if any, wisdom based on experience. From the experience of homeless youth we may be able to learn humility.

Watching children come into a soup kitchen and calmly go to the coffee pot to get a cup of coffee is an experience many rarely witness. Most of our reactions to children or adolescents drinking coffee would be shock. However, as we come to appreciate the cruelty under which some of these children survive we have to ask ourselves the question, "Maybe a hot cup of coffee is the greatest thing this youngster can do for himself in this moment in time?" Maybe this young person who last night slept outdoors and is wet from the rain just wants something hot to drink. Maybe, just maybe, I as an adult should support this effort rather than question it. Once again herein is humility.

Our eagerness to give to youngsters may take certain forms. We give them what we assume to be nutrition until we realize we have given a bag of items the young person is allergic to. Then comes the question, "Was my passion to be of assistance or was my passion to quell my own inner-uncomfortable feelings?" Humility is once again wrapped up in a psychic equation that possibly cannot be unraveled.

They are young people after all. Why can't I as an adult be their hero? Why is there no easy answer? Why is there no simple solution? Why do I feel vulnerable? Herein lies maybe an indispensable element of being human.

Originally we stated, given this situation, the best thing a well-meaning adult can do is to ask the question: "Is there any way I can be of assistance to you?"

This is a wonderful question because it is an admission of a reality that is bigger and more powerful than the adult asking the question. It is the admission of a reality with countless complexities beyond most of our comprehensions. When this question is asked of a homeless young person, or of any human being who is homeless, the feeling of humility that we feel in that moment is comparable to the feelings of humility the homeless live with daily. In that moment, whether we can be of assistance or not, is not as of great consequence when compared to the fact that we chose to share the feelings of vulnerability and humility with another human being. It is this sharing of human emotions that connects us and allows the homeless not to feel alone if even only in that moment.

The sharing of a moment is a present. In essence, it is the most valuable present one human being can give another.

I once heard the saying "the homeless shall always be with us." I sincerely hope not but if they are, then maybe that is their gift to society. They remind us of the fact that to be human is to be humble and vulnerable. Maybe in humility and vulnerability is some manner of nobility.

The homeless remind me of what Helen Keller said: "I long to accomplish a great and noble task, but it is my chief duty to accomplish humble tasks as though they were great and noble. The world is moved along, not only by the mighty shoves of its heroes, but also by the aggregate of the tiny pushes of each honest worker."

NINTH STORY

DREAMS IN THE SOUP KITCHEN

The typical fancy of a young person going off to college is maybe being dropped off by one's parents in a vehicle full of possessions for the young person to start the dream of a better life than his parents had; however it is not the reality of how some young folks start their college careers.

The homeless population that astonishes me most are those that choose to go to school in the midst of homelessness. Everyone I have met that has chosen this way has amazed me. These folks maintain in their hearts a castle in the sky. I am in awe of their flights of the imagination.

Harriet Tubman once remarked, "Every great dream begins with a dreamer. Always remember, you have within you the strength, the patience, and the passion to reach for the stars to change the world." I have always remembered this quote because during a ten-year span Harriet made nineteen trips into the South at the risk of death and escorted over three hundred slaves to freedom. She once mentioned to Frederick Douglass that she "never lost a single passenger."

These brave homeless souls who choose to further their education while in the midst of horrendous challenge remind me of Harriet, only more so, for the souls they are attempting to save are their own. They choose to better the world by bettering themselves. It requires courage to dream beyond one's foreseeable capacity.

One of these folks is Scott. If you met Scott on the streets you would not like him. He first grabbed my attention in the midst of a mild argument he was having while asking a librarian a question. By his speech I thought he lacked manners and/or normally reasonable verbal etiquette. He does! In addition, he was very much disheveled.

He was attempting to complete the paperwork to enter college and was having significant challenges obtaining the required documentation from Child Protective Services the system in which he grew up. We were sitting in a computer lab at the time and the librarian and I assisted him with his endeavor.

The second time I saw him was at the breakfast in the soup kitchen. Once again he was in the midst of a mild verbal altercation, however this time I viewed him differently, knowing this was a person who never had the benefit of something most of us take for granted: parents. I wondered how many lessons he may have missed out on and what skills were now lacking in him as a result.

Later that morning as I was handing out lunches to the homeless, he asked me for two lunches, since he was on his way to school. He had been accepted into college and this was his first day. I gave him three lunches and more congratulations than I have probably ever given before. Occasionally I still see him going through trash bins collecting the returnable bottles with a back-pack full of books on his back. He wants to be an engineer. He sometimes sleeps in the park, but often does something known as couch surfing.

He may wear his pants farther down his butt than I would personally consider appropriate, but I have come to admire this guy. He has a dream!

I know Marc better than I know Scott. He is in his sixth semester in college. He sleeps in abandoned buildings, on park benches, and also couch-surfs on friends' couches from time to time. He also is in the military reserves. He cannot afford to pay tuition, housing, and food all at the same time. He is another individual who amazes me. He does not come by the soup kitchen as often as Scott because he keeps a job in a fast-food restaurant so he can eat, but occasionally he does show up for a meal. This guy has shared stories of doing homework by candle-light.

If there is such a thing as an American Dream I personally do not know any individuals who exemplify such a dream more than these two young men, who if you met them on the streets you would more than likely avoid since they always need a haircut, and unkempt is a normal way of life, not to mention they always look tired. Probably because, unless I misjudge, what is in their hearts is admirable.

In the words of Eleanor Roosevelt, "The future belongs to those who believe in the beauty of their dreams."

TENTH STORY

The Soup Kitchen

The runaway is among those who evoke one of the most overwhelming responses among the homeless. I am forced to ask, what in this individual's experience is so horrendous that homelessness is a good choice? On one occasion I was privileged to get an answer. I still shudder at the shock of realizing this young woman was better off on the street than she was in what she described as home. The feelings, hopes, aspirations, and dreams of the homeless are countless and frequently heartbreaking. In this young lady's case it was not the dream that was overwhelming, it was the fact that such a young soul had clearly given up the dream that she could be loved. Her youthful appearance feels as if she was forced to grow up too soon due to viciousness. Ironic it is that such treatment often leads to the inhumaneness of homelessness.

There are a myriad of people whose lives have been changed by auto accidents at the soup kitchen. Some with wheel-chairs, crutches, walkers, or other mobility issues. What they all have in common is in a moment their lives were changed forever. There are many whose bodies are obviously impacted in both arms and legs on either the right or left side. Carol is one such woman, tall, slender, strikingly beautiful, and kind to a fault. I watched her eating and commented to her "Oh, you're a lefty, huh?" She smiled as she replied, "Yeah, but not really. I was born right-handed, but after the auto accident I had to learn how to use my left hand." I was struck by the difficulty of this challenge in a young life and the consequences of such an occurrence. Jesus, who has had the same experience, is one of the kindest gentlemen I have ever met, however he also was left with a permanent limp. While having the use of only one arm, this is a man whom I have observed on numerous occasions pouring coffee for other individuals who have two arms. I am unsure how people whose bodies will never be the same climb out of homelessness when the limbs they need to climb no longer work.

If there is a stereotype of a homeless woman, Robin would be the poster child for that view. Her weathered wrinkles obviously amassed over years of destitution. The cart she pulls behind her is organized to allow for survival on the streets. Her need for food may be superseded by other needs, yet she occasionally shows up at the soup kitchen for food. This is the woman who stopped me on the street, grabbed me by the elbow while gently turning me around to observe the beauty of a sunset as it slipped beyond the horizon. In this moment she starts to talk more that I have ever heard her speak. She describes for me how she goes to the hospital in the next town over once a month. I naturally assume it is going to be about some form illness, but as she states, "There is a female surgeon there who plays violin once a month in one of the public areas of the hospital." She tells me she attends every month because the beauty of the music makes her cry. While her description of beauty was shockingly beautiful in and of itself, I questioned how often I truly appreciate the beauty of life as much as this homeless woman does. That was a wonderful moment of humility for me for which I am grateful, and each time I see this woman at the soup kitchen I am reminded not only to make time for beauty, but that life has beauty.

One of the stand-outs of the homeless population, for lack of any other better way to describe them is what I would call the "well read." The library is a respite for many of the homeless, and those whose habit is reading are as impressive as any academician ever was. I am not talking about those who talk out of ego, but of those who have acquired a wealth of knowledge over a long period of homelessness and now that wealth becomes highly perceptible to even the most casual observer. There are those who have read all the books of James Patterson, David Baldacci, or Dean Koontz to those who have become expert on anything from the Middle East to a particular religion, historical period, or any number of subjects.

Out of all the homeless I have met there are none who have impressed me more than MJ. He has never once complained of his predicament. He has consistently smiled each and every time I have ever seen him. His bright eyes are constantly, searchingly curious. MJ of course is nine months old but he is still one of my favorites.

Homelessness is beyond comprehension. It is inclusive of those in abandoned buildings, lowland meadows, creek banks, beaches, highway underpasses, public parks, couch surfing, warming centers, cooling centers, shelters, and more. There are the transient, the recently out of jail, recently out of the hospital, out of work, under-employed, unemployed, the veteran, the runaway, the alcoholic, the addicted, the mentally ill, the abused, the terrorized, the temporarily disabled, the permanently disabled, those who have been beaten down by an unbearable life, and the terminal who are approaching the end of the journey. The youngest I have witnessed was three days old, the oldest somewhere in his eighties. Who among us comprehends this? There are mysteries and paradoxes we do not yet understand.

In this spirit the holidays are celebrated at the soup kitchen. The spirit of the unknown. The spirit of not knowing where the next meal may come from. The spirit of not knowing where one may lay one's head. The spirit of not feeling as if survival is guaranteed. Holidays are different among the homeless than it is for most in America. The meal in the soup kitchen is generally on paper plates or plastic or metal trays. It is a day for giving thanks, however the thanks given for the meal seems to have more meaning for those who do not know where the next meal is coming from or if it will come. This is most apparent in watching parents during a dinner in the soup kitchen. How does a parent encourage a three-year-old to eat when at the moment the child is just not hungry and the parent realizes that later in the day there will be no more food? There is gratitude because it did not rain when one sleeps outdoors, gratitude if is not too cold, gratitude for survival.

For the homeless there is no sense of belonging, security, identity, or roots, and emotional well-being is an abstract concept for many that was lost long ago.

I have attempted to be a scribe here for souls that rarely have a voice.

It is often awe-inspiring to listen to dreams, stories, and opinions of those who are in the midst of the struggle for survival and realize there are still dreams in those hearts.

There is life among the homeless. They are forced to be more loyal to the journey of life since they frequently lack the means to create the delusion or illusion of life that we create with a keen chase of the enjoyable, pleasant, or gratifying that often fills much of our lives. They are forced to be unconditionally present to what is and more accepting of the vicissitudes that are a part of the journey. If endurance is a virtue, it is self-evident in the homeless.

Life continues without a place to lay one's head. Life cannot be put on hold so it continues differently, in form and perspective even in a population that is often unseen. There is gentility and sacrifice in the face of a life of cruel circumstances. It is a story of nobility that has deserved to be told.

If we are on some form of indescribable journey in pursuit of some manner of spiritual evolvement, then maybe the homeless serve a purpose in such an evolution. Although the task of survival occupies much of their time, the diversity of the journey cannot strengthen or lessen a journey none of us quite yet understand.

It has been an honor to attempt to reflect the hearts of some of creation's most vulnerable. If I have grown from the experience, it is in realizing that I do not know and in learning to simply always ask, "What next?"

Epilogue

I wish to give a complimentary word for the soup kitchens that serve the homeless. These are the hospitals/spiritual communities of the poor, the needy, and the destitute. As human organisms we have many aspects of existence and we cannot nurture one without consideration of the other.

ABOUT THE AUTHOR

I was born in Newark, New Jersey. Most of my childhood experiences were in Newark, Harlem, New York, and the Bronx; I am the eldest of three children.

As a teenager I read Langston Hughes, Erich Maria Remarque, Maya Angelou, Ernest Hemingway, Stephen Crane, Countee Cullen, W.E.B. Du Bois, Nathaniel Hawthorne, Lorraine Hansberry, Charles Dickens, Mark Twain, Gwendolyn Brooks, Amiri Baraka, Arna Bontemps, and Jack London, to name a few of my favorites. I considered all of the above to be great storytellers, however my father had six brothers. The seven brothers enthralled the child I once was with the power of their storytelling. I learned at an early age storytelling had the ability to transcend time and space. In my family there were stories of decades past where one could still smell the aroma of Georgia pine trees in the Bronx or the scent of apple pies cooked on stoves that burned wood long ago. I dreamed of being part of that community of storytellers and nothing makes me happier than a really good story.

I have always enjoyed writing from as long ago as I can remember, dating back to the first paper I wrote in college which was twelve typed pages entitled "Cross Elasticities of Black Collegiate Demand" that I wrote for an economics class.

I've lived in almost a dozen states and today I live in Escondido, California. I still possess a deep love for Tennessee, Kentucky, and Ohio. Or maybe those states remind me of enjoyable parts of the journey of my soul through life.

In my spare time I enjoy reading the newspaper by the ocean, playing piano, and I am still an avid reader. I have worked for several symphony orchestras during my life and enjoy classical music.

My first book was entitled "EARNING MY PARENTS' LOVE" Growing Up In Alcoholism, Violence, and Dysfunction, a story of a child growing up in these maladies told from a child's point of view, which is what makes it extraordinary and unique. I also do guest speaking engagements at hospitals for medical students interested in the effects of growing up in alcoholism, violence, and dysfunction.

My next soon-to-be-released book is entitled: "The Idea That My Parents Did the Best That They Could Pisses Me Off." This book although my third, is a follow-up to the first book. It highlights those feelings that most folks have who grew up in alcoholism, violence, and dysfunction have, yet rarely speak about since we live in a pedagogic society that tends to sacrifice the true feelings of children.

www.ingramcontent.com/pod-product-compliance
Lightning Source LLC
Chambersburg PA
CBHW050548280326
41933CB00011B/1762